General Instructi

You probably already have most of the supplies needed for these projects. Even so, here are a few tips on materials and tools, general assembly instructions and finishing tips you may find helpful.

Basic Tools & Supplies

- Scissors for paper and fabric
- Rotary cutter, ruler and mat
- Nonpermanent fabric-marking tools
- Template material
- Sewing machine
- Walking or even-feed foot (optional)
- Hand-sewing needles
- Straight pins and pincushion
- Curved safety pins for basting
- Seam ripper
- Steam/dry iron and ironing surface

Fabric & Thread

For best results, use only good-quality 100 percent cotton fabric and quality thread. Your time is worth it. If you are prewashing, do so with ALL of the fabrics being used. Generally, prewashing is not required in quilting.

Fusible Web With Paper Release

There are a lot of appliquéd projects in this book, and all have been made using fusible web with paper release and machine blanket-stitched edges. Always follow the manufacturer's directions for fusing times as brands do vary. Of course, if you prefer to hand-appliqué or use other methods of machine appliqué, feel free to do so.

Batting

Almost any low or mid-loft batting will work for these projects. For items that will be subjected to heat, such as hot pads and coasters, using one or two layers of cotton batting along with needle-punched insulated batting is suggested.

A needle-punched insulated batting reflects heat and cold back to the source. This breathable material has deep fibers that prevent conduction and a reflective metalized film that prevents radiant energy from passing through. **Do not add this batting in anything you will be using in the microwave.**

Fabric Glue

Fabric glue is an optional item, as you can choose to tack the pieces in place by hand. But sometimes, it is easier and more practical to use glue. When using a fabric glue, apply it carefully and sparingly, and follow the manufacturer's directions.

Walking or Even-Feed Foot

A walking or even-feed foot attachment for your sewing machine is a very helpful tool when sewing layers, and it is useful for simple quilting patterns as well. This foot feeds the upper and lower layers of fabric through the machine at the same rate.

Pinking Shears

Since a lot of the projects have curved pieces that are sewn and turned, consider adding pinking shears to your toolbox if you don't already have a pair. If you cut around curved seams with the pinking shears, you eliminate the need to clip the curves with straight-edge scissors, saving time and effort. Pinking shears can also be used to control fraying on seam edges.

General Assembly Instructions

Read all instructions carefully before beginning each project.

All seams are ¼" unless otherwise directed.

The measurements given for each project include the outer seam allowance.

Press each seam as you sew.

Embroidery Embellishments

Some appliqués include simple embroidery stitches to complete the embellishments. Besides the embroidery thread listed in the materials list, be sure to have a good embroidery needle with a sharp point and an elongated eye on hand.

Transferring Patterns

Use a sharp pencil or an air-, water- or heat-soluble pen to transfer or trace the lines of embroidery patterns to a project's fabric.

Place the pattern, printed right side up, on a window or light box, and then layer the fabric on top, right side up. Trace the embroidery pattern.

You can also use a transfer, graphite or dressmaker's carbon paper to trace the lines.

Place the fabric on a smooth, hard surface. Top with the transfer paper, color side down, and then the pattern. Trace over the lines with a stylus or ballpoint pen to transfer.

Embroidery Stitches

The following embroidery stitches have been used in this book as embellishment.

Running Stitch

The running stitch is a simple in-and-out stitch that is the basis for all hand sewing. To work the stitch, run the needle in and out of the fabric at regular intervals. When instructions call for a gathering stitch, make long running stitches and pull on the thread to gather the fabric.

Running Stitch

Backstitch

The backstitch is used for outlining and lettering. Bring the needle and thread up at 1 and take a small backstitch to 2. Then bring it out again, one stitch length ahead, at 3. The space between 1 and 2 and between 1 and 3 should be the same. Continue to make backstitches into the hole of the previous stitch. ***Note:*** *When a pattern line has sharper curves, use a smaller stitch length to stay on the lines.*

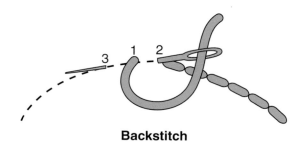

Backstitch

French Knot

To make a French knot, bring the needle and thread up at 1. Hold the thread taut and wrap it around the needle twice; then pull it gently to keep the wraps snug but not too tight. Keeping the tension, insert the needle back into the fabric at 2, about one thread away from position 1. Push the loops down the needle to lie on top of the fabric and then pull the needle through carefully.

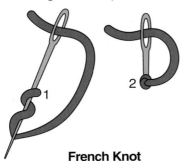

French Knot

Yo-Yo's

Yo-yo's are used in several projects and are an easy-to-make fabric embellishment.

Appliqué

Many of the projects in this book are made using fusible web with paper release and a machine blanket stitch. Refer to Raw-Edge Fusible Appliqué on page 6 for specifics. Other appliqué methods may be substituted if desired. All of the appliqué patterns are reversed so they will face the correct direction when fused to the background. When appliqués overlap, slip one edge under the other ¼" before fusing.

Sometimes, appliqué fabric is so light-colored or thin that the background fabric shows through excessively. You can correct this transparency problem by fusing a piece of lightweight interfacing to the wrong side of the fabric and then applying the fusible web with the marked pattern to the interfacing side. Cut out and use in the same way.

To add dimension to appliqué pieces, use the padded appliqué method, a technique in which batting is sewn into the appliqué shape. Refer to Padded Appliqué on page 7 for specifics on using this method.

Making Yo-Yo's

To make any size yo-yo:

1. Trace size circle desired or indicated on pattern using a template on wrong side of fabric.

2. Cut a length of thread in a color to match fabric; double thread and knot ends together.

3. Working with wrong side of yo-yo circle facing you, turn fabric under ¼" to wrong side and insert needle near the folded edge as shown in Figure A.

Figure A

4. Stitch a running stitch, using approximately ⅜"-long stitches, around the edge of the circle, turning fabric edge under as you sew referring to Figure B. Stop stitching when you reach the beginning knot.

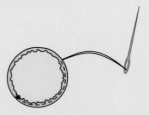

Figure B

5. Pull thread to gather the circle as tightly as you can (or as desired) and move the hole to the center of the circle as seen in Figure C.

Figure C

6. Insert needle between two gathers to the back of the yo-yo and make several small knots to secure; clip thread.

Raw-Edge Fusible Appliqué

One of the easiest ways to appliqué is the fusible-web method. Paper-backed fusible web motifs are fused to the wrong side of fabric, cut out and then fused to a foundation fabric and stitched in place by hand or machine. You can use this method for raw- or turned-edge appliqué.

1. If the appliqué motif is directional, it should be reversed for raw-edge fusible appliqué. If doing several identical appliqué motifs, trace reversed motif shapes onto template material to make reusable templates.

2. Use templates or trace the appliqué motif shapes onto paper side of paper-backed fusible web. Leave at least ½" between shapes. Cut out shapes leaving a margin around traced lines.

3. Follow manufacturer's instructions and fuse shapes to wrong side of fabric as indicated on pattern for color and number to cut.

4. Cut out appliqué shapes on traced lines and remove paper backing from fusible web.

5. Again following manufacturer's instructions, arrange and fuse pieces on the foundation fabric referring to appliqué motif included in pattern.

6. Hand- or machine-stitch around edges. ***Note:*** *Position a light- to mediumweight stabilizer behind the appliqué motif to keep the fabric from puckering during machine stitching.* Some stitch possibilities are satin or zigzag, buttonhole, blanket or running stitch.

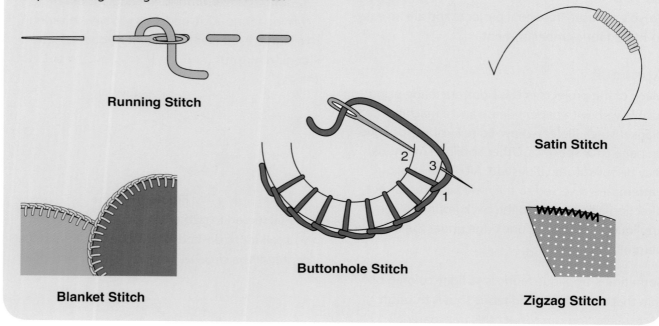

Running Stitch

Satin Stitch

Blanket Stitch

Buttonhole Stitch

Zigzag Stitch

Padded Appliqué

Some of the projects are finished with a "padded" appliqué. In this technique, an appliqué piece is sewn with two layers of fabric and a layer of batting and then turned right side out through an opening. Padded appliqué gives dimensional interest to a project.

1. Prepare template using pattern provided and trace the shape on the wrong side of the selected fabric. Fold the fabric in half with the right sides facing and the traced shape on top.

2. Pin this fabric to a scrap of batting that is slightly larger than traced shape and then sew on the traced lines as shown in Figure A.

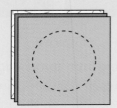

Figure A

3. The instructions will tell you whether you should leave a side opening for turning in the seam allowance, or if you should sew all around and then make a slash in one layer of fabric only for turning.

4. Cut out the shape ⅛"–¼" from the seam line, clip curves generously (or use pinking shears to cut out).

5. To make a slash, pinch the top layer of fabric and pull away that layer from the other fabric layer; make a little snip in the pinched fabric. Insert scissor tips into the hole and cut the fabric just enough to turn the shape right side out (Figure B). If desired, add a little no-fray solution to the cut edges of the slash and let it dry.

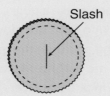

Figure B

6. After turning the shape right side out through the slash or side opening, whipstitch the cut edges of slash back together as shown in Figure C or slip-stitch the side opening closed. Press the shape from the top side so it is flat and smooth at the edges.

Figure C

Finishing Your Quilts

Prepare batting and backings larger than the quilt top. For bed-size quilts, we suggest battings and backings that are 8" larger than the quilt. For smaller projects, refer to materials lists for sizes.

Quilting

1. Press quilt top on both sides and trim all loose threads.

2. On a flat surface, make a quilt sandwich by layering the backing right side down, the batting on top of the backing and then the quilt top centered right side up on the batting. Make sure each layer is smoothed out. Pin or baste layers together to hold.

3. Use nonpermanent marking tool to mark quilting design on quilt top. Quilt as desired by hand or machine. *Note: If you are sending a bed-size quilt to a professional quilter, contact quilter for specifics about preparing your quilt for quilting.*

4. When quilting is complete, remove pins or basting. Trim batting and backing edges even with raw edges of quilt top.

Binding

1. Join binding strips on short ends with diagonal seams to make one long strip; trim seams to ¼" and press seams open (Figure 1).

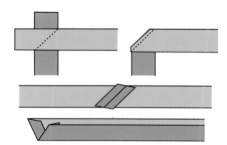

Figure 1

2. Fold 1" of one short end to wrong side and press. Fold the binding strip in half with wrong sides together along length, again referring to Figure 1; press.

3. Starting about 3" from the folded short end of the binding, sew binding to quilt-top edges, matching raw edges and using a ¼" seam. Stop stitching ¼" from corner and backstitch (Figure 2).

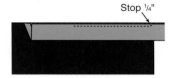

Figure 2

4. Fold binding up at a 45-degree angle to seam and then down even with quilt-top edge, forming a pleat at the corner, referring to Figure 3.

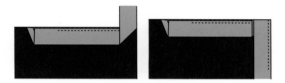

Figure 3

5. Resume stitching from corner edge as shown in Figure 3, down quilt side, backstitching ¼" from next corner. Repeat, mitering all corners, stitching to within 3" of starting point.

6. Trim binding end long enough to tuck inside starting end and compete stitching (Figure 4).

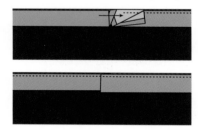

Figure 4

7. Fold binding to quilt back and stitch in place by hand or machine to complete your quilt. ●

Signs of Fall Pot Holders

Add a touch of fall to your kitchen with this trio of cute and functional pot holders.

Skill Level
Confident Beginner

Finished Size
Pot Holder Size: 7½" x 7½" excluding embellishments

Materials
- Scraps brown, green and cream batiks
- ⅓ yard or fat quarter each red, yellow and red-orange print batiks
- 6 (8") squares cotton batting plus scraps
- 3 (8") squares insulated batting
- Thread
- 6 (³⁄₁₆") black buttons
- 6 small plastic rings
- Thread
- Fusible web with paper release
- Basic sewing tools and supplies

Project Notes
Read all instructions before beginning this project.

Stitch right sides together using a ¼" seam allowance unless otherwise specified.

Refer to General Instructions on page 3 for specific construction and appliqué tips and techniques.

Materials and cutting lists assume 40" of usable fabric width.

Cutting
Prepare a template using the Sunflower Center 1 pattern given in the insert.

From brown batik:
- Cut 1 (⅞" x 4½") E strip.
- Cut 1 Sunflower Center 1 using prepared template.

From cream batik:
- Cut 3 (3½") B squares, 1 (3") D square and 4 (2¼") G squares.

From red batik:
- Cut 1 (8") F square and 1 (8") backing square.

From yellow batik:
- Cut 1 (8") H square and 1 (8") backing square.

From red-orange print batik:
- Cut 2 (3½") A squares, 3 (3") C squares and 1 (8") backing square.

Assembling the Maple Leaf Pot Holder

Refer to the Placement Diagram and project photo throughout for positioning of pieces.

1. Draw a diagonal line from corner to corner on the wrong side of two B squares.

2. Layer one each A and B square right sides together and stitch ¼" on each side of marked line. Cut apart on the marked line and press open to make two A-B units (Figure 1). Repeat to make a total of four A-B units. Trim each unit to 3" square, keeping seam centered in corners.

Figure 1

3. Cut the remaining B square in half diagonally.

4. Matching centers, sew a B triangle to one long side of the E strip referring to Figure 2; press toward E strip. Sew the remaining B triangle to the opposite side of E (Figure 3); press toward E.

Figure 2   **Figure 3**

5. Referring to Figure 4, trim B-E unit to 3" square with E centered.

Figure 4

6. Arrange the A-B units, B-E unit and C and D squares into three rows of three units each. Sew the units and squares together in three rows and then sew the rows together to complete the pot holder top.

7. Position the red-orange print backing square with the pot holder top, right sides facing, and layer on top of one insulated batting square, shiny side down, and two cotton batting squares; pin layers to secure. Sew around edges leaving a 3-inch opening in one side. Trim corners, grade seam allowance and turn right side out. Fold in seam allowance of opening and slip-stitch closed. Press edges flat and smooth.

8. Topstitch ¼" from edge. Quilt as desired.

9. Sew plastic rings to the top back corners for hanging.

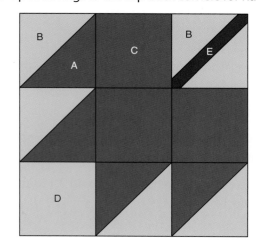

Maple Leaf Signs of Fall Pot Holder
Placement Diagram 7½" x 7½"

Assembling the Apple Pot Holder

Refer to the Placement Diagram and project photo throughout for positioning of pieces.

1. Draw a diagonal line from corner to corner on the wrong side of each G square.

2. With right sides together, pin a G square onto each corner of F square referring to Figure 5.

Figure 5

3. Referring to Figure 6, stitch on the drawn line on each G square; trim seam to ¼".

Figure 6   **Figure 7**

4. Flip G triangles out as shown in Figure 7; press seams toward G triangles.

5. Prepare templates using patterns listed and provided on the insert for this pot holder: Stem 3 and Leaf 4.

6. Referring to Padded Appliqué instructions on page 7, make one brown batik stem and one green batik leaf, leaving the straight end of the stem open for turning.

7. Topstitch ¼" from edges of stem. With top of stem facing toward the center of the pot holder, baste the stem to the front center top of the apple with raw edges matching.

8. Repeat steps 7 and 8 of Assembling the Maple Leaf Pot Holder, using the red batik backing square and pulling stem up and away from pot holder front after turning it right side out.

9. Position the leaf on the apple, near the base of the stem and stitch vein lines referring to Leaf 4 pattern to attach the center of the leaf to the apple.

10. Sew plastic rings to the top back corners for hanging.

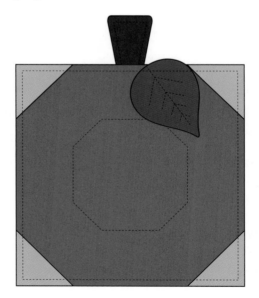

Apple Signs of Fall Pot Holder
Placement Diagram 7½" x 7½"
excluding embellishments

Assembling the Sunflower Pot Holder

Refer to the Placement Diagram and project photo throughout for positioning of pieces.

1. Repeat steps 7 and 8 of Assembling the Maple Leaf Pot Holder, using the H square and yellow batik backing square.

2. Prepare Sunflower Petal 1 template using pattern provided on the insert for this pot holder.

3. Referring to Padded Appliqué instructions on page 7, make nine yellow batik petals, leaving straight ends open for turning. After turning, stitch three lines on each petal as indicated on pattern.

4. Arrange the nine petals referring to Figure 8 in a circle on the pot holder front with the petals pointing outward. The inside circle should measure 2¾" across.

Figure 8

5. Pin in place or use fabric glue to hold in place. Stitch a circle catching the raw petal edges in place to secure.

6. Place the brown sunflower center to cover the raw petal edges and hand-stitch in place, turning the circle edges under as you stitch.

7. Sew the six black buttons to the sunflower center, catching the back of the pot holder with the stitches.

8. Sew plastic rings to the top back corners for hanging. ●

Sunflower Signs of Fall Pot Holder
Placement Diagram 7½" x 7½"
excluding embellishments

Fall's Here! & Scaredy-Cat Table Runners

With a switch in appliqués you can celebrate both autumn and Halloween. The Scaredy-Cat table runner has a black-and-white checkerboard center that can be used for games, and the pattern includes a bag for storing button "checkers."

Skill Level
Confident Beginner

Finished Size
Table Runner Size: 38" x 12"

Project Notes
Read all instructions before beginning these projects.

Stitch right sides together using a ¼" seam allowance unless otherwise specified.

Refer to General Instructions on page 3 for specific construction and appliqué tips and techniques.

Materials and cutting lists assume 40" of usable fabric width.

Fall's Here! Table Runner

Materials
- Scraps black solid, green batik and assorted autumn-color batiks
- ⅜ yard orange batik
- ⅜ yard brown batik
- ½ yard cream batik
- Backing to size
- Batting to size
- Thread
- Cream embroidery floss
- Fusible web with paper release
- Basic sewing tools and supplies

Cutting

From assorted autumn-color batiks:
- Cut 32 (2") A squares.

From brown batik:
- Cut 1 (1½" by fabric width) strip.
  Subcut strip into 2 (1½" x 12½") C strips.
- Cut 3 (2¼" by fabric width) binding strips.

From cream batik:
- Cut 1 (12½" by fabric width) strip.
  Subcut strip into 2 (12½") B squares.
- Cut remainder of 12½" strip into 5 (2" x 15") strips.
  Subcut strips into 32 (2") A squares.

Assembling the Fall's Here! Table Runner
Refer to the Placement Diagram and project photo throughout for positioning of pieces.

1. Referring to Figure 1, alternate cream and autumn-color A squares into eight rows of eight squares each. Stitch the squares together in each row; press seams to one side, alternating direction from row to row.

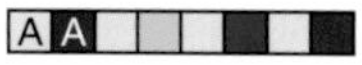

Figure 1

2. Sew rows together to finish the checkerboard center (Figure 2); press.

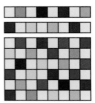

Figure 2

3. Prepare appliqué templates using patterns listed and provided on the insert for this table runner: Crow Wing, Crow Body, Pumpkin 1, Stem 1 and Leaf 2.

4. Trace appliqué shapes onto paper side of fusible web referring to list below for number to trace and cut out. Apply shapes to wrong side of fabric as listed below.

- Orange batik: 2 Pumpkin 1
- Brown batik: 2 Stem 1
- Green batik: 2 Leaf 2
- Black solid: 2 Crow Wing and 2 Crow Body

5. Cut out appliqué shapes and remove paper backing. Arrange pumpkins 1" from bottom of each B square. Slip stem under the top of the pumpkin and position leaves and crows with wings on pumpkins. Fuse in place.

6. Machine blanket-stitch around each appliqué shape using matching thread.

7. Sew C strips to opposite sides of the checkerboard center; press seams toward C.

8. Sew appliquéd squares to C strips to complete the runner top; press seams toward C.

Completing the Fall's Here! Table Runner

1. Layer, quilt and bind referring to General Instructions on page 3.

2. Model was quilted around each appliqué. Using green thread, quilt curvy tendrils and vein lines on leaves. Use orange thread to quilt contour lines down each pumpkin and double-stitch crow legs with black thread.

3. Make a French knot for each crow's eye with two strands of cream embroidery floss referring to the General Instructions on page 5.

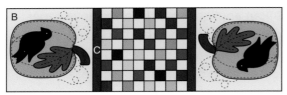

Fall's Here! Table Runner
Placement Diagram 38" x 12"

Scaredy-Cat Table Runner

Materials

- Scrap brown batik
- ¼ yard cream solid
- ½ yard black with tan speckles
- ⅝ yard black solid
- ⅝ yard orange batik
- Backing to size
- Batting to size
- Thread
- 12" length orange No. 3 pearl cotton
- 4 (³⁄₁₆") cream buttons
- 2 (¼") orange buttons
- 8 each 1" black and tan flat buttons for checkers
- Fusible web with paper release
- Basic sewing tools and supplies

Cutting

From cream solid:
- Cut 2 (2" by fabric width) strips.
  Subcut strips into 4 (2" x 17") E strips.

From black with tan speckles:
- Cut 1 (12½" by fabric width) strip.
  Subcut strip into 2 (12½") G squares.

From black solid:
- Cut 1 (7" by fabric width) strip.
  Subcut strip into 1 (7" x 9") H rectangle.
- Cut 2 (2" by fabric width) strips.
  Subcut strips into 4 (2" x 17") D strips.

From orange batik:
- Cut 1 (1½" by fabric width) strip.
  Subcut strip into 2 (1½" x 12½") F strips.
- Cut 3 (2¼" by fabric width) binding strips.

Assembling the Scaredy-Cat Table Runner
Refer to the Placement Diagram and project photo throughout for positioning of pieces.

1. Alternating colors, sew four each D and E strips together on long sides to make a strip set as shown in Figure 3; press seams toward E strips.

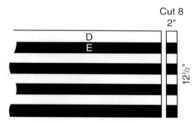

Figure 3

2. Subcut the strip set into eight 2" x 12½" segments, again referring to Figure 3.

3. Arrange segments in a checkerboard pattern and sew together to complete the checkerboard center; press.

4. Prepare appliqué templates using patterns listed and provided on the insert for this table runner: Pumpkin 1, Stem 1, Eye 1, Scaredy-Cat Body, Scaredy-Cat Head and Round Mouth.

5. Trace appliqué shapes onto paper side of fusible web referring to list below for number to trace and cut out. Apply shapes to wrong side of fabric as listed below.

- Orange batik: 2 Pumpkin 1
- Brown batik: 2 Stem 1
- Black solid: 2 Scaredy-Cat Body, 2 Scaredy-Cat Head, 2 Round Mouth and 4 Eye 1 (reverse 2)

6. Cut out appliqué shapes and remove paper backing. Arrange pumpkins 1" from bottom of each G square. Slip stem under the top of the pumpkin and position cat over pumpkin so legs extend ½" below pumpkin. Position pumpkin eyes and mouth on pumpkin. Fuse in place.

7. Machine blanket-stitch around each appliqué shape using matching thread.

8. Sew F strips to opposite sides of the checkerboard center; press seams toward F.

9. Sew appliquéd squares to F strips to complete the runner top; press seams toward F.

Completing the Scaredy-Cat Table Runner
1. Layer, quilt and bind referring to General Instructions on page 3.

2. Model was quilted around each appliqué. Use orange thread to double-stitch contour lines down each pumpkin and cream thread to double-stitch cat whiskers.

3. Sew cream buttons to the cat faces as eyes and the orange buttons at the center of whiskers for noses.

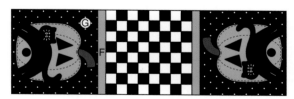

Scaredy-Cat Table Runner
Placement Diagram 38" x 12"

Completing the Checker Bag

1. Prepare appliqué templates using patterns listed and provided on the insert for this checker bag: Small Pumpkin and Stem 4.

2. Trace appliqué shapes onto paper side of fusible web referring to list below for number to trace and cut out. Apply shapes to wrong side of fabric as listed below.

• Orange batik: 1 Small Pumpkin
• Brown batik: 1 Stem 4

3. Cut out appliqué shapes and remove paper backing. Referring to Figure 4, arrange pumpkin 1" from side and ¾" from bottom edge of H rectangle. Slip stem under pumpkin. Fuse in place.

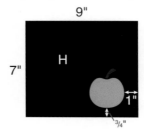

Figure 4

4. Machine blanket-stitch around each appliqué shape using matching thread.

5. Fold H rectangle in half, right sides facing, so it measures 4½" x 7". Stitch a ¼" seam down the long edge and across the bottom. Turn bag right side out and press.

6. Sew a double ¼" hem at the open end.

7. Using orange pearl cotton, start 1" down from hemmed edge and sew a long running stitch referring to General Instructions on page 4. Leave tails at both beginning and end to gather top of bag and tie into a bow as shown in Figure 5. ●

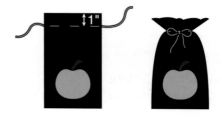

Figure 5

Harvesttime Tea Towels

Some simple appliqué, a couple of towels and a bit of hand embroidery are all you need to make this apple-themed pair.

Skill Level
Beginner

Finished Size
Tea Towel Size: Size varies

Materials
- Scraps black with tan speckles, and tan, red, brown and green batiks
- 1 each red and tan purchased tea towel
- Thread
- Black No. 8 pearl cotton or embroidery floss
- Fusible web with paper release
- Basic sewing tools and supplies

Project Notes
Read all instructions before beginning these projects.

Stitch right sides together using a ¼" seam allowance unless otherwise specified.

Refer to General Instructions on page 3 for specific construction and appliqué tips and techniques.

Completing the Tea Towels
Refer to the Placement Diagrams and project photos throughout for positioning of pieces and stitching.

1. Prewash, dry and press tea towels.

2. Prepare appliqué templates using patterns listed and provided on the insert for these tea towels: Stem 2, Leaf 3, Apple, Pie Pan and Pastry.

3. Trace appliqué shapes onto paper side of fusible web referring to list below for number to trace and cut out. Apply shapes to wrong side of fabric as listed below.

- Black with tan speckles: Pie Pan and 1 (¾" x 12") strip for ledge
- Tan batik: Pie Pastry
- Red batik: 3 Apples
- Brown batik: 3 Stem 2
- Green batik: 3 Leaf 3

Be Thankful Harvesttime Tea Towel
Placement Diagram size varies

Apples Harvesttime Tea Towel
Placement Diagram size varies

4. Cut out appliqué shapes and remove paper backing. Arrange pie pan and pastry in the center at one end of the red tea towel referring to Figure 1; arrange apples, stems, leaves and ledge strip in the center at one end of the tan tea towel referring to Figure 2.

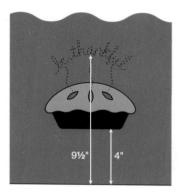

9½"   4"

Figure 1

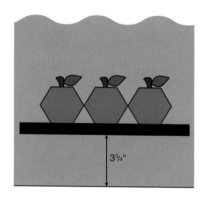

3¾"

Figure 2

5. Fuse appliqués in place. Machine blanket-stitch around each appliqué shape using matching thread.

6. Using embroidery design provided and Pastry pattern, transfer "be thankful" embroidery letters and steam lines above the pie, referring again to Figure 1 for placement, and use one strand of black pearl cotton or three stands of black embroidery floss to embroider words using an outline stitch referring to the General Instructions on page 4. ●

Pumpkin Panache Mug Rugs

This pumpkin has the option to be made as is or
add the face to create a jack-o'-lantern.

Skill Level
Confident Beginner

Finished Size
Mug Rug Size: 8¼" x 11" including stem

Materials
Materials and cutting instructions are for
one mug rug.
- Scraps brown batik and black solid
  (Halloween only) or green batik
  (autumn only)
- 1 (10" x 18") rectangle orange batik
- 1 (9" x 10") rectangle cotton batting
  plus scraps
- 1 (9" x 10") rectangle insulated batting
- Thread
- Fusible web with paper release
- Basic sewing tools and supplies

Project Notes
Read all instructions before beginning this project.

Stitch right sides together using a ¼" seam
allowance unless otherwise specified.

Refer to General Instructions on page 3 for specific
construction and appliqué tips and techniques.

Completing the Halloween Mug Rug
Refer to the Placement Diagram and project photo
throughout for positioning of pieces.

1. Prepare templates for Stem 1 and Pumpkin 1
using patterns provided in the insert for this project.

2. Layer cotton batting with insulated batting on
top, shiny side up. Fold orange batik rectangle in
half with right sides together to make a 9" x 10"
rectangle; place on layered battings. Referring to
Padded Appliqué on page 7 and Figure 1, prepare
the pumpkin, leaving a 3" opening at top when
sewing for turning.

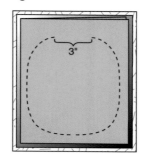

Figure 1

3. Again referring to Padded Appliqué instructions
on page 7, complete the stem using brown batik
and two layers of cotton batting. Topstitch ¼"
from the edge.

4. Slip the straight end of the stem inside the
pumpkin top opening. Fold in seam allowances on
the pumpkin opening, finger-press and slip-stitch
the opening closed, sewing through the stem to
catch it in the seam.

5. Topstitch ¼" from the pumpkin edge using matching thread.

6. Prepare appliqué templates using patterns listed and provided on the insert for this mug rug: Nose 1, Jagged Mouth and Eye 1.

7. Trace appliqué shapes onto paper side of fusible web referring to list below for number to trace and cut out. Fuse shapes to wrong side of fabric as listed below.

- Black solid: 1 Nose 1, 1 Jagged Mouth and 2 Eye 1 (reverse 1)

8. Cut out appliqué shapes and remove paper backing. Arrange appliqués on the front center of the pumpkin; fuse in place.

9. Machine blanket-stitch around each appliqué shape using matching thread. Quilt two contour lines as shown to complete the mug rug.

Completing the Autumn Mug Rug

1. Complete steps 1–5 of Completing the Halloween Mug Rug.

2. Prepare an appliqué template using the Leaf 2 pattern provided on the insert for this mug rug.

3. Trace appliqué shape onto paper side of fusible web referring to list below for number to trace and cut out. Apply shape to wrong side of fabric as listed below.

- Green batik: 1 Leaf 2

4. Follow steps 8 and 9 of Completing the Halloween Mug Rug, quilting vein lines in leaf. ●

**Halloween Pumpkin Panache
Mug Rug**
Placement Diagram 8¼" x 11"
including stem

**Autumn Pumpkin Panache
Mug Rug**
Placement Diagram 8¼" x 11"
including stem

Harvest Blessings Mug Rug

Having time to sit and have a cup of coffee or tea with a little snack is a blessing, and this mug rug will remind you to do just that.

Skill Level
Confident Beginner

Finished Size
Mug Rug Size: 11" x 8"

Materials
- Scraps orange and assorted autumn-color batiks
- Fat quarter each cream and green batiks
- 1 (8½" x 11½") rectangle cotton batting
- 1 (8½" x 11½") rectangle insulated batting
- Thread
- 3" length of ⅜"-wide green grosgrain ribbon
- Black No. 12 pearl cotton or embroidery floss
- Fusible web with paper release
- Craft glue (optional)
- Basic sewing tools and supplies

Project Notes
Read all instructions before beginning this project.

Stitch right sides together using a ¼" seam allowance unless otherwise specified.

Refer to General Instructions on page 3 for specific construction and appliqué tips and techniques.

Cutting
Prepare a circle template using the Pumpkin Yo-Yo pattern given in the insert.

From orange batik:
- Cut 1 yo-yo circle using prepared template.

From cream batik:
- Cut 1 (9" x 12") A rectangle.

From green batik:
- Cut 2 (1¾" x 6") B strips, 2 (1¾" x 11½") C strips and 1 (8½" x 11½") backing rectangle.

Completing the Mug Rug
Refer to the Placement Diagram and project photo throughout for positioning of pieces.

1. Prepare appliqué template using Leaf 1 pattern provided on the insert for this mug rug.

2. Trace appliqué shapes onto paper side of fusible web referring to list below for number to trace and cut out. Apply shapes to wrong side of fabric as listed below.

- Assorted autumn-color batiks: 5 Leaf 1 (reverse 2)

Here's a Tip

This mug rug pattern could also be used as a mini quilt wall hanging or could be attached to a bread basket for the table.

3. Using a nonpermanent marking tool and referring to Figure 1, center and mark a 9" x 6" rectangle on the right side of the A rectangle. Transfer the "harvest blessings" embroidery design to the marked rectangle, positioning the "h" 1⅝" from the left marked line and ⅞" down from the top line.

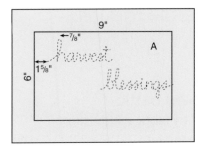

Figure 1

4. Embroider letters with one strand black pearl cotton or two strands black embroidery floss using a running stitch referring to the General Instructions on page 4.

5. When embroidery is complete, redraw 9" x 6" lines to compensate for shrinkage and cut out on lines; press.

6. Referring to Figure 2, stitch B strips to the short sides of A; press seams toward B.

Figure 2

7. Again referring to Figure 2, stitch C strips to top and bottom of B-A-B; press seams toward C.

8. Layer mug rug front and backing rectangle, right sides facing, on the cotton batting rectangle and insulated batting rectangle, shiny side down; pin layers to secure. Sew around edges, leaving a 3" opening in one side. Trim corners and turn right side out. Fold in seam allowance of opening and slip-stitch closed. Press edges flat and smooth.

9. Topstitch ¼" from the embroidered center into the border and ¼" from outside edge.

10. Cut out appliqué shapes prepared in step 2 and remove paper backing. Arrange appliqués on the mug rug center; fuse in place.

11. Machine blanket-stitch around each leaf using matching thread and stitch a vein line down the center of each leaf.

12. Referring to Making Yo-Yo's on page 5, use the orange circle to make a yo-yo but pull the hole to one side instead of the center (Figure 3a). Tie a knot at the center of the green ribbon and slip one end into the yo-yo hole (Figure 3b). Tack in place or secure with craft glue.

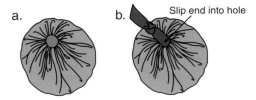

Figure 3

13. Position the yo-yo pumpkin on the mug rug under the word "harvest" and hand-stitch in place. ●

Harvest Blessings Mug Rug
Placement Diagram 11" x 8"

Pumpkin Stack Place Mat & Napkin Holder

Set a fun table theme on your table this fall.

Skill Level
Confident Beginner

Finished Sizes
Place Mat Size: 16" x 12"
Napkin Holder Size: 6" x 2" open

Materials
Materials and cutting instructions are for a set of 2 each place mats and napkin holders.
- Scraps orange and green batiks
- ½ yard brown batik
- ⅝ yard cream batik
- Backing to size
- 2 (12½" x 16½") rectangles cotton batting plus scraps
- Thread
- 8" (¼"-wide) green grosgrain ribbon
- 5" white elastic cord
- 2 (¼") green buttons
- 2 (¾") cream buttons
- Fusible web with paper release
- Basic sewing tools and supplies

Project Notes
Read all instructions before beginning these projects.

Stitch right sides together using a ¼" seam allowance unless otherwise specified.

Refer to General Instructions on page 3 for specific construction and appliqué tips and techniques.

Materials and cutting lists assume 40" of usable fabric width.

Cutting

From brown batik:
- Cut 1 (1½" by fabric width) strip.
  Subcut strip into 2 (1½" x 12½") C strips.
- Cut 4 (2¼" by fabric width) binding strips.

From cream batik:
- Cut 1 (12½" by fabric width) strip.
  Subcut strip into 2 (5½" x 12½") A rectangles and 2 (10½" x 12½") B rectangles.
- Cut 1 (2½" by fabric width) strip.
  Subcut strip into 4 (2½" x 6½") D strips.

Assembling the Place Mats
Refer to the Placement Diagram and project photo throughout for positioning of pieces.

1. Prepare appliqué templates using patterns listed and provided on the insert for this place mat: Leaf 1, Stem 4, Small Pumpkin, Middle Pumpkin and Bottom Pumpkin.

2. Trace appliqué shapes onto paper side of fusible web referring to list below for number to trace and cut out. Apply shapes to wrong side of fabric as listed below.

- Orange batik: 2 each Small Pumpkin, Middle Pumpkin and Bottom Pumpkin
- Brown batik: 2 Stem 4
- Green batik: 4 Leaf 1

3. Cut out appliqué shapes and remove paper backing. Referring to Figure 1, arrange appliqués vertically on an A rectangle with the bottom pumpkin 1" above edge of fabric. Tuck a stem end under the small pumpkin at top and position leaves. Fuse in place. Repeat with second A rectangle and remaining appliqué shapes.

Figure 1

4. Machine blanket-stitch around appliqués using matching thread.

5. Stitch a C strip to the left side of appliquéd panel; press seam toward C. Repeat to make two A-C units.

6. Stitch a B rectangle to the C side of each A-C unit; press toward C.

7. Layer, quilt and bind referring to General Instructions on page 8. Model was quilted around each appliqué and a crosshatch pattern was quilted on B. Double-stitched lines were quilted using green thread for the leaf vein lines and curly tendrils around the pumpkins.

Pumpkin Stack Place Mat
Placement Diagram 16" x 12"

Assembling the Napkin Holders

1. Cut elastic cord in half.

2. Referring to Figure 2, fold one elastic cord in half and baste ends to the right-side short end of a D strip.

Figure 2

3. With right sides of a plain D strip and an elastic D strip together, with elastic in between, pin D strips to a batting scrap. Sew ¼" from the edge all around, leaving a 2" opening on one side.

4. Trim corners and batting close to seam and then turn right side out, pulling out the elastic loop. Fold seam allowance to inside and slip-stitch closed.

5. Topstitch all around holder ¼" from edge.

6. Repeat steps 2–5 to make a second napkin holder.

7. Referring to Padded Appliqué instructions on page 7, draw and make two small pumpkins.

8. Cut the grosgrain ribbon in half. Referring to Figure 3, fold each ribbon length in half forming a loop and then flip ends up and back at an angle.

Figure 3

9. Sew a green button to the fold and attach to the top of each small pumpkin.

10. Position small pumpkin on center front of each napkin holder and quilt a circle in the middle through all layers.

11. Sew a cream button ⅜" from the left end on each napkin holder. ●

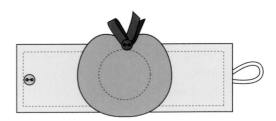

Pumpkin Stack Napkin Holder
Placement Diagram 6" x 2" open

Pumpkin Centerpiece & Name-Card Holders

Fabric pumpkins with matching name cards will make the perfect final touch to your next fall dinner gathering.

Skill Level
Confident Beginner

Finished Sizes
Centerpiece Sizes: 8" diameter, 6" diameter and 5" diameter excluding embellishments

Name-Card Holder Size: 3" diameter excluding embellishments

Materials
Materials and cutting instructions are for 1 set of 3 centerpiece pumpkins and 2 name-card holders.
- Fat quarter green batik
- 1½ yards orange batik
- Thread
- Plastic foam balls: 1 each 8", 6" and 5" diameter for centerpieces, and 2 (3") diameter for holders
- Wood sticks: 1 (1" x 3½") and 2 each ½" x 3" and ⅜" x 2"
- Orange hand-quilting or extra-strong thread
- 36" (18-gauge) green plastic-covered wire
- Wire cutters
- Large sheet of pattern paper
- Cardstock
- Serrated knife
- Craft glue
- Fusible web with paper release
- Decorative straight pins
- Basic sewing tools and supplies

Project Notes
Read all instructions before beginning these projects.

Stitch right sides together using a ¼" seam allowance unless otherwise specified.

Refer to General Instructions on page 3 for specific construction and appliqué tips and techniques.

Materials and cutting lists assume 40" of usable fabric width.

Cutting

From green batik:
- Cut 1 (13" x 20") A rectangle.

From wire:
- Cut 2 each 7", 6" and 5" lengths.

From fusible web:
- Cut 1 (10" x 13) rectangle.

Completing the Centerpieces & Name-Card Holders
Refer to the Placement Diagrams and project photos throughout for positioning of pieces.

1. Use serrated knife to slice a flat surface on each ball as shown in Figure 1. The flat area should measure approximately 4½", 3½" and 3¼" respectively across the three centerpiece balls and 2" across the name-card holder balls.

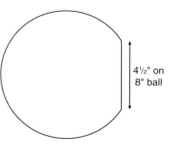

4½" on 8" ball

Figure 1

2. Referring to Figure 2, push the largest stick approximately ¾" into the center top of the 8" ball. Remove the stick, apply craft glue to the end and reinsert into the hole. Repeat for each ball, using smaller sticks.

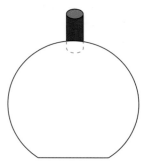

Figure 2

3. Using a tape, measure the 8" ball from the edge of the stick, down one side, across the bottom and up to the opposite side of the stick. Add 1¼" to the measurement to calculate the size of fabric circle needed.

4. Fold the large sheet of pattern paper into quarters and measure out from the folded corner half the circle diameter determined in step 3. Referring to Figure 3, make a number of marks at this distance and connect the dots to form a quarter-circle. Cut out along the curved line. Unfold the paper for the full-size pattern. Cut one circle this size from the orange batik.

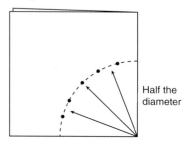

Half the diameter

Figure 3

5. Repeat steps 3 and 4 with each size of remaining balls and cut out a fabric circle from orange batik for each ball.

6. To cover the 8" ball, thread a needle with a double length of orange quilting thread; knot one end. Finger-press a ½" hem around the edge of the

circle as you sew a ⅜"-long gathering stitch near the fold. Refer to General Instructions on page 4 for sewing a gathering stitch. Continue stitching until you reach the beginning knot.

7. Place the ball flat side down inside the fabric circle and pull the gathering thread, bringing the fabric up to cover the ball. Continue to pull and arrange the fabric until it is tight around the stick. Knot the thread securely and clip.

8. Repeat steps 6 and 7 for the remaining balls and fabric circles using a ¼"-long gathering stitch.

9. Position the fusible web on the wrong side of A rectangle aligning one 13" side of the fusible web with the 13" side of A. Fuse in place and remove the paper backing.

10. Fold the other half of the A rectangle over so the web is sandwiched between the two fabric layers. Fuse.

11. Prepare templates using patterns listed and provided on the insert for the centerpiece and name-card holder: Leaf 2 and Leaf 7.

12. Using a nonpermanent marking tool, trace two each of each leaf shape with vein lines onto the prepared A piece (Figure 4).

Figure 4

13. With matching thread, start at the bottom of each leaf and stitch on the traced lines to outline the leaf. Double-stitch the vein lines.

14. Cut out each leaf a scant ⅛" outside the stitching lines and remove marks.

15. Referring to Figure 5, center a 7" wire length on the back of each large leaf and whipstitch the wire to the stitched vein line trying not to stitch though the front of the leaf. *Note: If needed, a few drops of glue may be used to secure the wire.*

Figure 5

16. Repeat with 5" wire lengths on the small leaves.

17. Apply glue to the bare wire end of a large leaf and insert it into the 8" pumpkin, near the stick. Repeat with the second large leaf on the opposite side. Insert one small leaf into each of the 6" and 5" pumpkins.

18. Referring to Figure 6, curl one end of a 6" length of wire. Repeat with the second 6" length.

Figure 6

19. Apply glue to the straight end and push it into the ball beside the stick of each name-card holder pumpkin.

20. Write names on small cardstock rectangles and use decorative pins to attach to the name-card holder pumpkins. ●

Large Pumpkin Centerpiece
Placement Diagram 8" diameter
excluding embellishments

Pumpkin Name-Card Holder
Placement Diagram 3" diameter
excluding embellishments

Small Pumpkin Centerpiece
Placement Diagram 5" diameter
excluding embellishments

Medium Pumpkin Centerpiece
Placement Diagram 6" diameter
excluding embellishments

Welcome Fall Wreath

This wreath has fabric leaves that bend, ribbon and
a quilted pumpkin to complete the look.

Skill Level
Confident Beginner

Finished Size
Wreath Size: 12" diameter, excluding embellishments

Materials
- Scrap brown batik
- Fat eighth orange batik
- 8 fat eighths of batiks in assorted autumnal leaf colors
- Cotton batting
- Thread
- 12"-diameter grapevine wreath
- 2⅔ yards 2½"-wide wire-edged fall print fabric ribbon
- 1 yard 26-gauge wire
- 1⅓ yards 18-gauge wire
- Wire cutters
- Fusible web with paper release
- Craft glue or low-temperature hot-glue gun
- Basic sewing tools and supplies

Project Notes
Read all instructions before beginning this project.

Refer to General Instructions on page 3 for specific construction and appliqué tips and techniques.

Cutting

From each leaf-color batik:
- Cut 1 (7" x 10") A rectangle.

From 18-gauge wire:
- Cut 8 (6") lengths.

From fusible web:
- Cut 8 (4¾" x 7") rectangles.

Completing the Embellishments

1. Position a fusible web rectangle on the wrong side of an A rectangle aligning one 7" side of the fusible web with one 7" side of A. Fuse in place and remove the paper backing.

2. Fold the other half of the A rectangle over so the web is sandwiched between the two fabric layers. Fuse.

3. Repeat steps 1 and 2 with the remaining A rectangles and fusible web rectangles.

4. Prepare templates using patterns listed and provided on the insert for this wreath: Leaf 2, Stem 7 and Pumpkin 2.

5. Using a nonpermanent marking tool, trace the Leaf 2 shape and vein lines onto each of the prepared A pieces, reversing the template for half of the leaves.

6. With matching thread, start at the bottom of each leaf and stitch on the traced lines to outline the leaf. Double-stitch the vein lines.

7. Cut out each leaf a scant ⅛" outside the stitching lines and remove marks.

8. Referring to Figure 1, center an 18-gauge wire length on the back of each leaf and whipstitch the wire to the stitched vein line trying not to stitch though the front of the leaf.

Figure 1

9. Repeat with all eight leaves. ***Note:*** *If needed, a few drops of craft glue may be used to secure the wire.*

10. Refer to Padded Appliqué instructions on page 7 to make one pumpkin using orange batik and one stem using brown batik, leaving the straight end of the stem open for turning.

11. If desired, quilt a few lines in the stem.

12. Fold in the seam allowance on the top of the pumpkin and insert the open end of the stem inside. Slip-stitch the folded edges of the opening closed, sewing through the stem to catch it in the seam.

13. Quilt contour lines within the pumpkin, if desired.

14. To make the bow, find the center of the ribbon length and fold two loops with the tails; squeeze the middle and wrap with 26-gauge wire to secure (Figure 2).

Figure 2

15. Continue to fold loops, two or more at a time, and wrap tightly with wire until you have eight loops and two ribbon tails approximately 12" long each. Do not trim wire.

Assembling the Wreath

Refer to the Placement Diagram and project photo throughout for positioning of pieces.

1. Place the bow on the wreath front and attach using the wire ends.

2. Finger-pleat and squeeze the ribbon together in two places on each streamer.

3. Push the pleated ribbon between the wreath vines allowing the ribbon to puff up between the pleated sections.

4. Position the pumpkin on the wreath and arrange the leaves by pushing the stem wires between the wreath vines.

5. When satisfied with the placement, glue the ribbon pleats, pumpkin and leaf stems in place.

6. Curl the leaves in a natural manner using the wire insets. ●

Welcome Fall Wreath
Placement Diagram 12" diameter
excluding embellishments

Here's a Tip

The pumpkin in this wreath is the perfect size for a coaster. Just make the pumpkin as directed and a leaf, such as Leaf 4 from Signs of Fall Pot Holders as an accent. Many times a part of a project can be used for something else with little or no alteration.

Little Brown Jug Wall Hanging

Let this little wall hanging announce the arrival of fall.

Skill Level
Confident Beginner

Finished Size
Wall Hanging Size: 15" x 26"

Materials
- Scraps green, gold, rust and dark brown batiks and black solid
- Fat eighth brown batik
- 3/8 yard dark taupe batik*
- 2/3 yard cream batik*
- Backing to size
- Batting to size
- Thread
- Cream embroidery floss
- 5 (1/2") cream buttons
- Fusible web with paper release
- Basic sewing tools and supplies

*Model was constructed using 1 yard of a gradated batik that contains both cream and dark taupe colors.

Project Notes
Read all instructions before beginning this project.

Stitch right sides together using a 1/4" seam allowance unless otherwise specified.

Refer to General Instructions on page 3 for specific construction and appliqué tips and techniques.

Materials and cutting lists assume 40" of usable fabric width.

Cutting
Prepare a 2½" circle template using the Yo-Yo Circle pattern given in the insert.

From dark taupe batik:
- Cut 2 (2½" by fabric width) strips.
  Subcut strips into 2 (2½" x 19½") C strips and 2 (2½" x 15½") D strips.
- Cut 1 (4½" by fabric width) strip.
  Subcut strip into 3 (4½") B squares.

From cream batik:
- Cut 3 (2¼" by fabric width) binding strips.
- Cut 1 (11½" by fabric width) strip.
  Subcut strip into 1 (11½" x 19½") E rectangle, 3 (4½") A squares and 5 yo-yo circles using prepared template.

Here's a Tip
Varying borders is a fun way to add a little more interest to a design. Not all four borders have to be the same width or color. Adding an extra border such as the hourglass row at the bottom of this wall hanging adds some zip without distracting from the main focus

Assembling the Appliqué Center
Refer to the Placement Diagram and project photo throughout for positioning of pieces.

1. Prepare appliqué templates using patterns listed and provided on the insert for this wall hanging: Jug, Jug Handle, Jug Inside Section, Crow Wing, Crow Body, Sunflower Petal 2, Sunflower Center 2, Stem 5, Leaf 5 and Sunflower Half-Center.

2. Trace appliqué shapes onto paper side of fusible web referring to list below for number to trace and cut out. Apply shapes to wrong side of fabric as listed below.

- Brown batik: 1 Jug and 2 Jug Handles (reverse 1)
- Dark brown batik: 1 Jug Inside Section
- Green batik: 3 Leaf 5 (reverse 1) and 2 Stem 5 (reverse 1 for short stem)
- Rust batik: 1 Sunflower Center 2 and 1 Sunflower Half-Center
- Gold batik: 15 Sunflower Petal 2
- Black solid: 1 Crow Wing and 1 Crow Body

3. Cut out appliqué shapes and remove paper backing. Arrange shapes on the E rectangle, starting with the jug centered 1" up from the bottom. Place ends of handles under jug as indicated on pattern. Slip stems between the jug and the inside section.

4. To arrange the full flower, lay out five petals in a circle (Figure 1a) and then place a second layer of five additional petals with tips between the bottom-layer petals (Figure 1b).

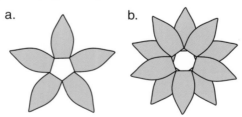

a.   b.

Figure 1

5. To create a half-flower, lay out two petals first and then overlap with three additional petals.

6. Add the flower centers and leaves. Position the crow and wing on the jug on the right-hand side.

7. When satisfied with the arrangement, fuse in place. Machine blanket-stitch around each appliqué shape using matching thread.

Completing the Wall Hanging

1. Sew C strips to opposite sides of the appliquéd E rectangle; press. Sew D strips to top and bottom; press.

2. Draw a diagonal line from corner to corner on the wrong side of each A square.

3. Layer one each A and B square right sides together and stitch ¼" on each side of marked line. Cut apart on the marked line and press seam open to make two A-B units (Figure 2). Press seam allowances open. Repeat to make a total of six A-B units.

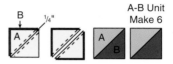

A-B Unit
Make 6

Figure 2

4. Draw a diagonal line on the wrong side of three A-B units, crossing the seam line.

5. Place a marked unit right sides together with an unmarked unit, matching dark to light in the layers (Figure 3). Stitch ¼" on each side of marked line. Cut units apart on the marked line and press seam open to make two triangle units. Repeat to make a total of six triangle units. Discard one triangle unit.

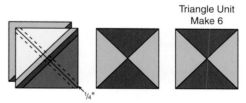

Triangle Unit
Make 6

Figure 3

6. Trim five triangle units to 3½" square to make five hourglass units, keeping seam centered in each corner (Figure 4).

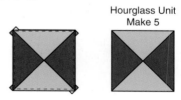

Hourglass Unit
Make 5

Figure 4

7. Arrange and stitch hourglass units into a horizontal row referring to Placement Diagram for color placement; press.

8. Sew hourglass row to the bottom D strip of wall hanging to complete the wall hanging top; press.

9. Follow the instructions for Finishing Your Quilts in General Instructions on page 8 to layer, quilt and bind.

10. The model wall hanging was quilted around each appliqué with a line down the center of each leaf and a line connecting each leaf to a stem using green thread. Using gold thread, quilt lines in the flower petals. Double-stitch the crow's legs using black thread.

11. Make a French knot with two strands of cream embroidery floss for the crow's eye as shown in General Instructions on page 5.

12. Follow Making Yo-Yo's on page 5 to make five yo-yo's from the 2½" cream circles. Sew a button to the center of each yo-yo, using the same thread to stitch the yo-yo to the center of each hourglass unit. ●

Little Brown Jug Wall Hanging
Placement Diagram 15" x 26"

Bat Treats Halloween Mug Rug

Sit and have a treat with your coffee. Take a break.

Skill Level
Confident Beginner

Finished Size
Mug Rug Size: 10" x 8"

Materials
- Scrap black solid
- Fat eighth beige batik
- Fat quarter purple batik
- 1 (8½" x 10½") rectangle cotton batting
- 1 (8½" x 10½") rectangle insulated batting
- Thread
- Purple No. 12 pearl cotton or embroidery floss
- 2 (³⁄₁₆") purple buttons
- Fusible web with paper release
- Basic sewing tools and supplies

Project Notes
Read all instructions before beginning this project.

Stitch right sides together using a ¼" seam allowance unless otherwise specified.

Refer to General Instructions on page 3 for specific construction and appliqué tips and techniques.

Cutting

From beige batik:
- Cut 1 (8" x 8") A square.

From purple batik:
- Cut 1 (2" x 4½") B strip, 1 (3" x 4½") C strip, 1 (2" x 10½") D strip, 1 (3" x 10½") E strip and 1 (8½" x 10½") backing rectangle.

Completing the Mug Rug
Refer to the Placement Diagram and project photo throughout for positioning of pieces.

1. Prepare appliqué templates using patterns listed and provided on the insert for this mug rug: Bat Body and Bat Wing.

2. Trace appliqué shapes onto paper side of fusible web referring to list below for number to trace and cut out. Apply shapes to wrong side of fabric as listed below.

- Black solid: 1 Bat Body and 2 Bat Wings (reverse 1)

3. Using a nonpermanent marking tool and referring to Figure 1, center and mark a 6½" x 4½" rectangle on the right side of the A rectangle. Transfer the "treats" embroidery design in the insert, positioning the first "t" ¾" from the left marked line and 1½" up from the bottom line.

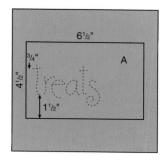

Figure 1

Here's a Tip

Because mug rugs are quick and easy to make, use up scraps and have such personality, they are great fun for exchanges within quilt guilds, sewing clubs or online groups.

treats

4. Embroider letters with one strand purple pearl cotton or two strands purple embroidery floss using a backstitch referring to the General Instructions on page 4.

5. When embroidery is complete, redraw 6½" x 4½" lines to compensate for shrinkage and cut out on lines; press.

6. Referring to Figure 2, stitch B strip to the left side and C to the right side of A; press seams toward border strips.

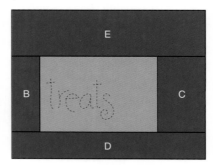

Figure 2

7. Again referring to Figure 2, stitch D to the bottom and E to the top of A-B-C; press seams toward border strips.

8. Layer mug rug front and backing rectangle, right sides facing, on the cotton batting and insulated batting rectangles, shiny side down; pin layers to secure. Sew around edges, leaving a 3" opening in one side. Trim corners and turn right side out. Fold in seam allowance of opening and slip-stitch closed. Press edges flat and smooth.

9. Topstitch ¼" from the embroidered center into the border and ¼" from outside edge.

10. Cut out appliqué shapes prepared in step 2 and remove paper backing. Arrange appliqués on the top right side of mug rug, slipping ends of wings under body, overlapping the inside panel and border; fuse in place.

11. Machine blanket-stitch around the bat with black thread.

12. Sew purple buttons to the bat for eyes. ●

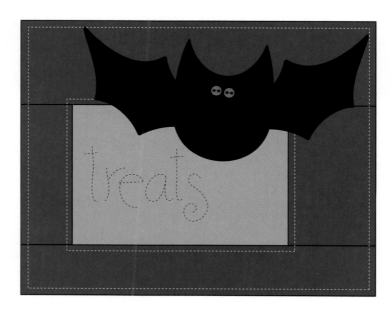

Bat Treats Halloween Mug Rug
Placement Diagram 10" x 8"

Pincushions for the Season

This trio of pincushions could also double for autumn decorations if you use your imagination.

Skill Level
Confident Beginner

Finished Sizes
Sunflower Pincushion Size: 3½" x 6"
Pumpkin Pincushion Size: 3" x 4½"
Black Cat Pincushion Size: 5" x 8"

Project Notes
Read all instructions before beginning these projects.

Stitch right sides together using a ¼" seam allowance unless otherwise specified.

Refer to General Instructions on page 3 for specific construction and appliqué tips and techniques.

Materials and cutting lists assume 40" of usable fabric width.

Sunflower Pincushion

Materials
- Scraps gold, brown and green batiks
- Cotton batting scraps
- Thread
- Polyester or cotton fiberfill
- 1 (⅞" x 2¾") wooden spool
- 1 (¾"-thick x ⅞"-diameter) round of cardboard with cork cover
- 6 (³⁄₁₆") black buttons
- 1 (¾") green button
- Green paint or stain (optional)
- Craft glue
- Basic sewing tools and supplies

Cutting
Prepare templates for Medium Circle 3 and Sunflower Petal 1 using patterns provided in the insert for this pincushion.

From brown batik:
- Cut 1 Medium Circle 3.

Completing the Pincushion
Refer to the Placement Diagram and project photo throughout for positioning of pieces.

1. Referring to Padded Appliqué instructions on page 7 and Figure 1, use Sunflower Petal 1 template and gold batik to make eight gold petals, leaving the straight end of each open for turning. After petals are turned right side out, stitch three lines in each petal using dark gold thread.

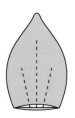

Figure 1

2. If desired, paint or stain the wooden spool; let dry.

3. Arrange four petals around the top of the spool referring to Figure 2a; glue in place. Arrange remaining four petals on top, staggering the position (Figure 2b); glue in place.

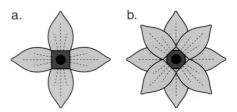

Figure 2

4. Using doubled thread and referring to General Instructions on page 4, sew gathering stitches ¼" from the edge of brown circle. Place a ball of fiberfill inside the center of the circle and top with the cardboard round, cork side toward the fiberfill. Gather the fabric over the edge of the cardboard. Add more fiberfill if needed to make the flower center firm. Gather tightly and knot.

5. Sew black buttons to the top of the brown flower center.

6. Glue the flower center on top of the flower petals.

7. Referring to Padded Appliqué instructions on page 7, use green batik and Sunflower Petal 1 template to make one leaf, leaving straight end open for turning. After turning right side out, fold in the seam allowance and whipstitch the opening closed. Quilt vein lines in leaf as desired.

8. Sew the green button to the straight end of leaf. Glue the leaf in place on wooden spool.

Here's a Tip

Adding fun novelty pins is an easy and especially nice touch when the pincushion is a gift. Buttons, ribbon flowers, plastic mini-shapes or other small embellishments all work nicely when glued to the top of a flat-head straight pin.

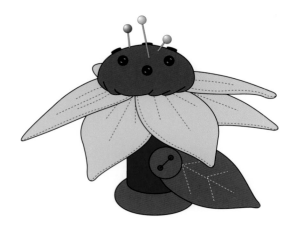

Sunflower Pincushion for the Season
Placement Diagram 3½" x 6"

Pumpkin Pincushion

Materials
- Scrap green batik
- ¼ yard orange batik
- Thread
- Polyester or cotton fiberfill
- Orange No. 12 pearl cotton or hand-quilting thread
- 1 (¾") domed, round shank button, any color
- 1 (¾") flat round orange button
- Long doll-making needle
- Basic sewing tools and supplies

Cutting

Prepare templates for Cover Button 1, Small Circle 2, Medium Circle 3 and Large Circle 4 using patterns provided in the insert for this pincushion.

From green batik:
• Cut 1 Cover Button 1 circle.

Completing the Pincushion

Refer to the Placement Diagram and project photo throughout for positioning of pieces.

1. Draw one each of Small Circle 2, Medium Circle 3 and Large Circle 4 on the wrong side of the orange batik, leaving at least ½" between shapes.

2. Fold fabric in half, right sides facing, with the drawn circles on top. Sew around the marked lines, leaving a 1½" opening on each circle. Cut out each circle ¼" from stitching, clip curves and turn right side out.

3. Stuff each circle firmly with fiberfill. Fold in seam allowance on each opening and slip-stitch folded edges closed.

4. Using one strand of orange pearl cotton or two strands orange quilting thread, tie a firm knot about 3" from one end of a 4-foot length. Referring to Figure 3, insert the needle into the center bottom of the large circle and come out at top center.

Figure 3

5. Wrap the thread around the edge of the circle and stitch up through the bottom center. Make a second wrap opposite the first and continue around the circle until eight equal sections are wrapped

(Figure 4) pulling the thread snugly after each wrap to indent the edges. Bring the needle down beside the beginning knot and tie to the 3" loose end to finish.

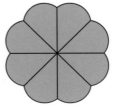

Figure 4

6. Repeat steps 4 and 5 to wrap the small and medium circles.

7. Stack the wrapped circles from largest to smallest to form a pumpkin shape. With a knotted length of pearl cotton or quilting thread, stitch from the top down through the center of the small circle, the center of the middle circle and then the center of the large circle.

8. Referring to Figure 5, stitch through two holes of the orange button, then reinsert needle into the bottom of the large circle and proceed back up through to the top of the small circle. Pull thread tightly to secure and indent the top and bottom circles; knot, but do not trim thread (Figure 6).

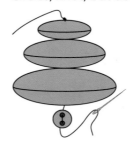 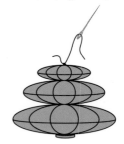

Figure 5   **Figure 6**

9. Using doubled thread and referring to General Instructions on page 4, sew gathering stitches ¼" from the edge of green cover button 1 circle. Place shank button, domed side down, in the center of the fabric circle and pull the thread to gather edge around the shank. Sew covered button to the top of pumpkin to resemble a stem.

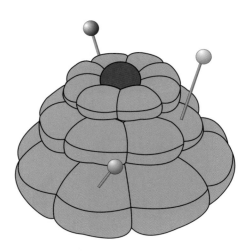

Pumpkin Pincushion for the Season
Placement Diagram 3" x 4½"

Black Cat Pincushion

Materials

- Scrap orange batik
- ¼ yard black solid
- Cotton batting scraps
- Thread
- Polyester or cotton fiberfill
- ½ yard 1½"-wide black-and-white wire-edge ribbon
- 4" (³⁄₁₆"-diameter) twine
- 1 cup crushed walnut shells or rice
- 2 (³⁄₈") cream buttons
- 3 flat-head straight pins
- 3 plastic Halloween spider embellishments
- Craft glue
- Basic sewing tools and supplies

Cutting

Prepare templates using patterns listed and provided on the insert for this pincushion: Black Cat Body, Black Cat Tail, Black Cat Base and Small Pumpkin.

From black solid:

- Cut 2 Black Cat Bodies, 2 Black Cat Tails and 1 Black Cat Base

Completing the Black Cat Pincushion

Refer to the Placement Diagram and project photo throughout for positioning of pieces.

1. Transfer markings from patterns to fabric pieces.

2. With right sides together, sew the two tail pieces together leaving open at the straight end. Clip curves and turn. Stuff lightly with fiberfill.

3. Referring to Figure 7, pin the tail to the right side of the cat body front and baste in place.

Figure 7

4. Pin the body front and back together with the tail sandwiched between. Stitch all around, leaving bottom seam and marked side area open. Clip curves but do not turn.

5. Pin body to the base, matching centers and aligning side seams with corresponding base markings.

6. Sew body and base together all around. Clip curves and turn right side out through side opening on body.

7. Pour crushed walnut shells or rice into the bottom of the body through opening. Firmly stuff remainder of body with fiberfill.

8. Fold in seam allowance on the opening and slip-stitch folded edges closed.

9. Referring to Figure 8, sew buttons to cat face for eyes. Trim twine to 3" length and tie a knot in the center. Glue or tack the knot to the face for a nose. Untwist twine ends for whiskers and trim as desired.

Figure 8

10. Wrap the ribbon around the cat's neck and tie in a bow at the side.

11. With right sides together, fold orange fabric in half and trace small pumpkin on top. Insert and pin remaining 1" twine length between the fabric layers so ¾" will extend at top for stem after seam is sewn. Sew all around edges. Cut out ¼" from the seam and clip curves. Make a slash through one layer of fabric only and turn right side out; press. Quilt circle or contour lines on pumpkin, as desired.

12. Apply glue to the slashed side of the pumpkin and place it on the front bottom edge of cat.

13. To make spider pins, glue plastic spiders to the flat top of the pins. ●

Black Cat Pincushion for the Season
Placement Diagram 5" x 8"

Here's a Tip

There are many materials that can be used to stuff pincushions—some better than others, especially if you plan on using the pincushion to keep your pins sharp and handy. Suggested materials include:

- *Polyester or cotton fiberfill*
- *Crushed walnut shells*
- *Rice*
- *Sterilized sand*
- *Emery*
- *Wool roving*

Personally, I prefer crushed walnut shells because they give weight to the pincushion so it doesn't move around too much and the residual oils in the shells help prevent rust. Rice also gives weight and helps absorb moisture. I often use shells or rice and finish with fiberfill.

Sometimes it is necessary to use a funnel to add the shells or rice. Cutting the bottom off a plastic water bottle makes a great funnel for this purpose. Insert the mouth of the bottle into the pincushion and pour the shells or rice into the pincushion's opening.

Boo Crew Wall Hanging

This fun and easy wall hanging will make all your visitors smile. No one will ever guess how easy it is to make.

Skill Level
Beginner

Finished Size
Wall Hanging Size: 22" x 14"

Materials
- Scraps brown and green batiks
- Scrap black solids
- Fat quarter cream batik
- ⅓ yard orange batik
- ½ yard purple batik
- Backing to size
- Batting to size
- Thread
- 2 (³⁄₁₆") purple buttons
- 2 (⁷⁄₁₆") black buttons
- 1 (½") cream button
- Fusible web with paper release
- Basic sewing tools and supplies

Project Notes
Read all instructions before beginning this project.

Stitch right sides together using a ¼" seam allowance unless otherwise specified.

Refer to General Instructions on page 3 for specific construction and appliqué tips and techniques.

Materials and cutting lists assume 40" of usable fabric width.

Cutting

From cream batik:
- Cut 1 (10½" x 18½") A rectangle.

From orange batik:
- Cut 2 (2½" by fabric width) strips.
  Subcut strips into 2 (2½" x 10½") B strips and 2 (2½" x 22½") C strips.

From purple batik:
- Cut 3 (2¼" by fabric width) binding strips.

Completing the Appliqué Center
Refer to the Placement Diagram and project photo throughout for positioning of pieces.

1. Stitch B strips to opposite short sides of A rectangle; press seams toward B.

2. Stitch C strips to top and bottom of A; press seams toward C.

3. Prepare appliqué templates using patterns listed and provided on the insert for this wall hanging: Letter B, Bat Wing, Bat Body, Stem 6, Leaf 6, Cat Eye, Cat Ear, Cat Head/Pumpkin, Smile, Nose 2 and Eye 2.

4. Trace appliqué shapes onto paper side of fusible web referring to list below for number to trace and cut out. Apply shapes to wrong side of fabric as listed below.

- Brown batik: 1 Stem 6
- Green batik: 2 Leaf 6
- Cream batik: 2 Cat Eye and 1 Smile
- Black solid: 1 Bat Body, 2 Bat Wings (reverse 1), 1 Cat Head, 2 Cat Ears, 2 Eye 2 (reverse 1), 1 Nose 2 and 1 Smile
- Orange batik: 1 Pumpkin
- Purple batik: 1 Letter B

5. Cut out appliqué shapes and remove paper backing. Arrange appliqués on the A rectangle referring to Figure 1, starting with letter B and the pumpkin. Slip stem under the top of the pumpkin.

6. Position the cat head in the middle, slightly overlapping the letter B and the pumpkin; tuck cat ears under the top of the cat head. Position the bat body on letter B. Tuck ends of the bat wings under the bat body and extend the left wing into the B strip and the tip of the right wing into the C strip. Fuse these appliqués in place.

7. Position cat eyes and smile on cat head; fuse in place. Position eyes, nose and smile on the pumpkin and add leaves; fuse in place.

8. Machine blanket-stitch around each appliqué shape using matching thread.

Completing the Wall Hanging

1. Follow the instructions for Finishing Your Quilts in General Instructions on page 8 to prepare for quilting.

2. The model wall hanging was quilted around each appliqué with curly tendrils extending from the pumpkin and leaves. Using cream thread, quilt whiskers on the cat. Using black thread, double-stitch lines through the cat's smile to suggest teeth.

3. When quilting is completed, refer to Finishing Your Quilts in General Instructions on page 8 for binding.

4. Sew purple buttons on the bat for eyes. Sew black buttons on cream circles for the cat eyes and a single cream button at center of the whiskers for the cat nose. ●

Figure 1

Boo Crew Wall Hanging
Placement Diagram 22" x 14"

My Favorite Color Is October Quilt

All the beautiful colors of fall come together in this stunning star quilt and the appliquéd leafy border is the perfect finishing touch.

Skill Level
Confident Beginner

Finished Sizes
Quilt Size: 56" x 70"
Block Size: 12" x 12"
Number of Blocks: 12

Materials
- 1¾ yards total assorted autumn-color batiks including brown, rust and gold
- ⅝ yard green batik
- 2⅓ yards black with tan speckles
- 2½ yards cream batik
- Backing to size
- Batting to size
- Thread
- 1½ yards fusible web with paper release
- Basic sewing tools and supplies

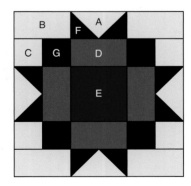

Maple Star
12" x 12" Finished Block
Make 12

Project Notes
Read all instructions before beginning this project.

Stitch right sides together using a ¼" seam allowance unless otherwise specified.

Refer to General Instructions on page 3 for specific construction and appliqué tips and techniques.

Materials and cutting lists assume 40" of usable fabric width.

Here's a Tip
The Maple Star block can be easily converted into a Maple Leaf block. Simply remove one B-C-G or reversed B-C-G unit and replace it with a 4½" cream batik square. Then add an appliquéd stem to the square.

Cutting

From assorted autumn-color batiks:
- Cut 12 sets of 4 (2½" x 4½") D rectangles (to total 48 D rectangles).*
- Cut 12 (4½") E squares.*
- Cut 20 (2½") I squares.
*Each Maple Star block in the model has 4 D rectangles around an E square in the same color but in a different shade.

From green batik:
- Cut 190" of 1⅜"-wide bias strips.

From black with tan speckles:

- Cut 4 (2⅞" by fabric width) strips.
  Subcut strips into 48 (2⅞") squares. Cut each square on one diagonal to make 96 F triangles.
- Cut 3 (2½" by fabric width) strips.
  Subcut strips into 48 (2½") G squares.
- Cut 11 (2½" by fabric width) strips.
  Subcut strips into 31 (2½" x 12½") H strips.
- Cut 7 (2¼" by fabric width) binding strips.

From cream batik:

- Cut 1 (58½" by fabric width) strip.
  Subcut strip into 2 (6½" x 58½") J strips and 2 (6½" x 56½") K strips.
- From remainder of 58½" strip, cut 2 (5¼" x 58½") strips.
  Subcut strips into 12 (5¼") squares. Cut each square on both diagonals to make 48 A triangles.
- Cut 3 (4½" by fabric width) strips.
  Subcut strips into 48 (2½" x 4½") B rectangles.
- Cut 3 (2½" by fabric width) strips.
  Subcut strips into 48 (2½") C squares.

Completing the Blocks

1. Sew an F triangle to the left angled edge of A (Figure 1a), matching bottom edges; press seam toward F (Figure 1b).

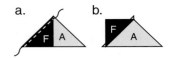

Figure 1

2. Sew an F triangle to the right angled edge of A (Figure 2a); press seam toward F (Figure 2b). Trim flying geese unit to measure 2½" x 4½".

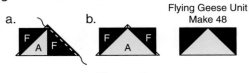

Figure 2

3. Repeat steps 1 and 2 to make a total of 48 flying geese units.

4. Referring to Figure 3, stitch one each C and G square together; press toward C. Repeat to make a total of 48 C-G units.

Figure 3

5. Sew a B rectangle to a C-G unit, referring to Figure 4 for orientation; press toward B. Repeat to make a total of 24 each B-C-G units and reversed B-C-G units, again referring to Figure 4.

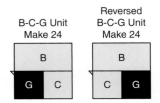

Figure 4

6. Referring to Figure 5 for orientation, sew a D rectangle to "point" end of a flying geese unit to make an A-F-D unit; press toward D. Repeat to make a total of 48 A-F-D units.

Figure 5

7. Referring to the block drawing for orientation, select two each B-C-G units and reversed B-C-G units, four matching A-F-D units and one E square in the same color family as the A-F-D units. Arrange units with E in three rows of three units each.

8. Sew units together to form rows; press seams in top and bottom rows outward and in the center row inward toward E.

9. Sew rows together to complete one Maple Star block; press.

10. Repeat steps 7–9 to make a total of 12 blocks.

Completing the Quilt Center

1. Referring to Assembly Diagram, stitch four H strips together with three blocks to make a row, beginning and ending with an H strip; press seams toward H. Repeat to make four rows.

2. Join three H strips and four I squares, starting with I squares and alternating placement to make a sashing row; press toward H. Repeat to make five sashing rows.

3. Stitch rows together to complete quilt center; press toward sashing rows.

Assembling Appliqué Borders

For ease of machine stitching, appliqué borders are prepared before sewing to the quilt center. All blanket stitching is completed except where appliqués cross border seams.

1. Prepare appliqué templates using patterns listed and provided on the insert for this quilt: Spool End, Leaf 2, Sunflower Petal 2 and Sunflower Center 2.

2. Trace appliqué shapes onto paper side of fusible web referring to list below for number to trace and cut out. Apply shapes to wrong side of fabric as listed below.

- Autumn-colored batiks: 18 Leaf 2 (reverse 8)
- Gold batik: 40 Sunflower Petal 2
- Rust batik: 4 Sunflower Center 2
- Brown batik: 4 Spool Ends
- Green batik: Draw 2 (2½" x 3¾") rectangles on fusible web for spools

3. Cut out appliqué shapes and remove paper backing.

4. Cut bias strip into two 41" and two 52" lengths. Fold the strips in half lengthwise, wrong sides together, and stitch a ¼" seam. Trim seam to ⅛". Referring to Figure 6, refold strip so the seam is centered on the back; press the seam open and edges flat to make four vine strips.

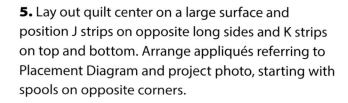

Figure 6

5. Lay out quilt center on a large surface and position J strips on opposite long sides and K strips on top and bottom. Arrange appliqués referring to Placement Diagram and project photo, starting with spools on opposite corners.

6. Referring to Figures 7 and 8, position and curve longer vines on side borders and shorter vines on top and bottom borders, placing ends of side vines under spools and ends of top and bottom vines on top of spools.

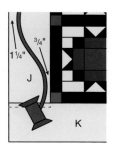

Figure 7

Figure 8

7. Layer sunflower petals as shown in Figure 9 and place sunflower centers over center of petals. Place sunflowers close to the end of each vine. Slip a leaf under each sunflower to cover the vine end. Position remaining leaves near the curves in the vines.

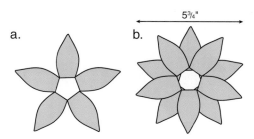

Figure 9

8. When satisfied with the arrangement, remove spools and spool ends. Fuse pieces in place except do not fuse vine ends that will overlap or go under the spools. Machine blanket-stitch around each appliqué shape using matching thread.

9. Sew J borders to opposite sides; press toward borders.

10. Sew K borders to top and bottom; press toward borders.

11. Reposition spools, spool ends and vine ends in the corners; fuse in place. Machine blanket-stitch as in step 8 to complete quilt top.

12. Follow the instructions for Finishing Your Quilts in General Instructions on page 8 to layer, quilt and bind the quilt. ●

Here's a Tip

Make four or five blocks and join them in a long row to make a striking table runner.

Here's a Tip

To make a bed-size quilt, make as many Maple Star blocks as needed to reach the desired size. Replace the appliquéd borders with a coordinating print, if desired.

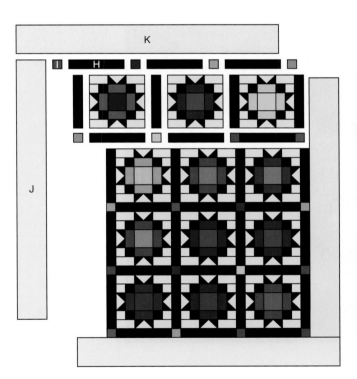

My Favorite Color Is October Quilt
Assembly Diagram 56" x 70"

My Favorite Color Is October Quilt
Placement Diagram 56" x 70"

Supplies

We would like to thank the following manufacturers who provided materials to make sample projects for this book.

Batik fabrics from SewBatik™.

Dream Cotton Select batting from Quilters Dream Batting.

Fusible web and fusible interfacing from Bosal.

Tea towels from Dunroven House.

In addition, the author would like to thank professional longarm quilter Jean McDaniel for her work on the My Favorite Color Is October quilt.

Annie's® *Harvest Time Quilting* is published by Annie's, 306 East Parr Road, Berne, IN 46711. Printed in USA. Copyright © 2016 Annie's.

RETAIL STORES: If you would like to carry this publication or any other Annie's publications, visit AnniesWSL.com.

Every effort has been made to ensure that the instructions in this publication are complete and accurate. We cannot, however, take responsibility for human error, typographical mistakes or variations in individual work. Please visit AnniesCustomerService.com to check for pattern updates.

ISBN: 978-1-59012-603-5

1 2 3 4 5 6 7 8 9

Introduction

*"Every leaf speaks bliss to me
Fluttering from the autumn tree."*

These few words from Emily Brontë pretty much sum up my feelings and images of autumn. It is a truly beautiful season, full of color and movement and interesting motifs such as pumpkins, sunflowers, crows and of course—always—the leaves. In addition, the fun "mini season" of Halloween is included with its cast of whimsical characters: black cats and bats, spiders and jack-o'-lanterns. It's no wonder that I enjoy designing for this time of year!

This book includes over 20 projects for your home to celebrate this colorful season. You will find everything from pincushions and pot holders to table decor, wall hangings, a wreath and a quilt. There are many techniques included to make the projects unique, techniques that you may find useful additions to your repertoire. So let's celebrate our fabulous fall!

Meet the Designer

Chris Malone has been sewing and crafting most of her life. As an accomplished sewist, quilter and designer, she has had hundreds of designs published in sewing and quilting publications and has authored several books of her own.

She is a regular contributor to *Quilter's World* magazine and Annie's quilting and sewing book titles. Chris' whimsical style has been a favorite of many quilters and sewists and is easily recognizable at a glance.

Chris resides in the diverse and beautiful Willamette Valley of Oregon.

Table of Contents